MOVIE POSTERS
The Paintings of Batiste Madalena

MOVIE POSTERS
The Paintings of Batiste Madalena

INTRODUCTION BY
Judith Katten

AN APPRECIATION BY
Anthony Slide

Harry N. Abrams, Inc., Publishers, New York

INTRODUCTION

Judith Katten

IN the early 1920s, George Eastman, the renowned photographic inventor, manufacturer, and philanthropist, decided to enrich the cultural life of his hometown, Rochester, New York. Believing that a well-appointed auditorium could attract leading international performers and musicians, Eastman set out to create a theater that would rival the best in the world. But he also envisioned his theater as a showcase for the newest form of popular entertainment — motion pictures. Indeed, a top-flight movie theater built by Eastman in downtown Rochester was supremely fitting. It was, after all, the success of this new medium that had made him a multimillionaire and Rochester a boom town. For it was the Eastman Kodak factories that manufactured the sprocketed film on which Hollywood captured the dream images that it exported around the world.

The creation of the Eastman Theater was no ordinary undertaking. Civic pride and Eastman's ego demanded the very best. Immersing himself in all aspects of the project, Eastman personally supervised even the smallest details. He selected leading architects to design an elaborate edifice, equipped with the most advanced lighting, sound, and projection technology. He chose as its site the lot adjacent to the four-year-old Eastman School of Music, whose student orchestra would perform at the theater, which opened in 1922.

One element that Eastman considered essential was the series of seven ornate polished brass cases flanking the theater's entrances. A master showman, he was particularly intent on reaching the public with alluring posters ballyhooing his theater's attractions. His dissatisfaction with the mass-produced posters supplied by the movie companies convinced Eastman that he had to create his own. They had to be beautiful, artistic yet enticing.

Eastman's advertising manager searched through the portfolios of talented local artists for the perfect candidate to meet this challenge. He found him in Italian-born Batiste Madalena, who was then in his early twenties. Upon graduation from the Mechanics Institute, a respected academy of art later renamed the Rochester Institute of Technology, Madalena had been awarded a scholarship by the Art Students League in New York City. But the opportunity to serve as Eastman's poster artist persuaded the young man to postpone his studies in New York.

And so began a remarkable and unique association. Eastman commissioned Madalena to paint original posters for his theater's display cases, art

The Eastman Theater in the 1920s with its row of brass poster cases

that would flash a message of excitement about the attractions within. Just as the new entertainment palace was extravagant and unusual, so too would be the posters that advertised its movies.

The relationship between artist and patron would last for four years. By 1928, when the mercurial Eastman (he was to commit suicide in 1932) decided to leave the theater business and leased his movie palace to the Paramount Publix chain, Madalena had created an estimated 1,400 paintings.

Given full creative rein, Madalena had only one directive — his paintings must be clearly visible from passing trolleys. Working mainly from stills and story synopses supplied by the movie companies, Madalena created an entirely distinctive body of work. Using tempera on poster board, he succeeded more often than not in capturing the essence of a movie in one striking image — and then creating six more variations on that theme.

Now in his eighties, the artist (who never did leave Rochester for New York after all) freely acknowledges the many influences on his work. Trained by teachers who had enjoyed exposure to European art, Madalena incorporated into his work the best of foreign influences. He often saw the movie studios' posters, and borrowed their illustrative devices when it served his purpose. But what made his work distinctive was his proficiency in executing a variety of styles with unfailing panache.

Posters for the dramas capture the eye most forcefully; for example, the striking images for *Laugh, Clown, Laugh,* starring Lon Chaney, commanded attention by means of stark contrasts, rich texture, and strong line. The posters for comedies, which Madalena now says he most enjoyed working on, were painted in a flat, unpretentious, almost "friendly" style, illustrated by those for *Rough House Rosie,* starring Clara Bow, where the warmth and humor of the subject is brightly conveyed. And for the epics, heroic films such as *The Ten Commandments,* Madalena was able to surmount the limitations of the posters' vertical format to render panoramas of sweep and power.

Considering the sheer volume of his output — he produced an average of eight posters each week — Madalena worked with amazing skill as well as speed. In the interest of expediency, he often resorted to the poster board itself as the background color, using a black board for the dramas, such as *The Covered Wagon,* while painting the comedy posters on light-colored boards, such as those used to advantage in *Lilac Time.* Evidence of the haste in which he worked is found in typographical errors in the hand lettering. Quotation marks were omitted and misspellings occurred on several posters, such as *The Way of All Flesh,* mistakes that would not have been permitted on the studio-produced work that was checked and rechecked before being printed.

Madalena's work differs most strikingly from the studio product in its freedom from a major burden, billing requirements. Mass-produced movie posters are cluttered with credits: stars, supporting cast, director, producer, associate producer, producing studio — by contract each had to be allocated precious space. Madalena chose to ignore all billing requirements in the interest of his art, using only those names that were helpful as a compositional or design element. Arbitrarily, Madalena might from time to time include a line of advertising copy, either from the studio's campaign or supplied by the Eastman advertising department, simply because a particular poster needed a typographic element. But for the most part he tolerated little intrusion into his art.

In 1928, shortly after Paramount Publix took over the Eastman Theater, Madalena, who was considered by the new management to be a dispensable extravagance, left to open his own commercial art studio in downtown Rochester. Without him, the theater's handsome display cases were filled with standard studio one-sheets, the same mass-produced posters that were plastered on billboards in every city and town across the country.

One rainy evening in the fall of 1928, Madalena decided to take a shortcut home from his studio through the back alley behind the Eastman Theater. Rounding the corner on his bicycle, the artist came upon a distressing sight. There in the rain lay hundreds of his paintings, unceremoniously dumped by the new management. Working frantically, he managed to carry some two hundred of his poster-paintings home where, working through the night and assisted by his wife, Margaret, he carefully dried and inspected each for damage. Even today, Madalena grows angry at the memory of how his work was discarded like so much trash. "I was so goddarn sore," he recalled in a recent interview. "Why didn't they say anything? I would have paid them for some of them."

After repairing the backs of the boards where they had begun to peel, pressing the damp posters with a warm iron, and flattening them under heavy books, Madalena carefully constructed crates in which to store the surviving pieces. And for fifty years, those crates remained untouched in his attic.

In 1973, the Lincoln Savings Bank of Rochester mounted an exhibition of the work of local artists in the lobby of its downtown branch. Included among the artists was Batiste Madalena. For the first time in half a century, the Madalena movie posters were on public view in Rochester. My husband, Steven, a documentary filmmaker then in Rochester attending a convention, happened to see the exhibition. Wandering into the bank lobby during a break in the convention proceedings, he was immediately captivated by the extraordinary quality of Madalena's work. Unable to put the powerful images out of his mind even after returning to Los Angeles, Steven finally telephoned the artist to inquire about purchasing some of the posters. Although several art galleries were interested in the work, Madalena agreed to sell the entire collection to us because we shared his desire to bring these wonderful pieces of Americana to the public's attention.

Happily, Josine Ianco-Starrels of the Municipal Art Gallery of Los Angeles, the first curator to whom we spoke, recognized the merit of the work and agreed to an exhibit. In May 1981, the movie poster-paintings of Batiste Madalena finally made it to Hollywood. William Wilson, art critic for the *Los Angeles Times*, in praising the works wrote in his review, "The selection of 50 (of the paintings) on view in Barnsdall Park . . . makes us glad the artist took a shortcut home that night."

Since that first Los Angeles exhibit, Madalena's poster-paintings have been shown in museums throughout California and in exhibits arranged by the Art Museum Association, a nonprofit organization that arranges traveling shows for its member museums. Supported by a grant from Warner Communications, they have been touring museums nationwide for the past three years. The story of the paintings and their rediscovery has also captured the imagination of the media, most notably of Charles Kuralt, who described the paintings on his "Sunday Morning" television show as " . . . the greatest movie posters ever created."

So it is that George Eastman's extravagance has finally been vindicated. The movie posters he commissioned have claimed their rightful place in this country's cultural and artistic history, affording us an appreciation of an era and a poster–art form long gone.

The Son of the Sheik

CAST
Rudolph Valentino, Vilma Banky, George Fawcett, Montague Love, Karl Dane

DIRECTOR
George Fitzmaurice

STUDIO
Feature Productions/United Artists

YEAR
1926

The Covered Wagon

CAST
Lois Wilson, J. Warren Kerrigan, Ernest Torrence

DIRECTOR
James Cruze

STUDIO
Famous Players — Lasky/Paramount Pictures

YEAR
1923

The Freshman

CAST
Harold Lloyd, Jobyna Ralston, Brooks Benedict

DIRECTOR
Sam Taylor, Fred Newmeyer

STUDIO
Harold Lloyd Corp. / Pathé Exchange

YEAR
1925

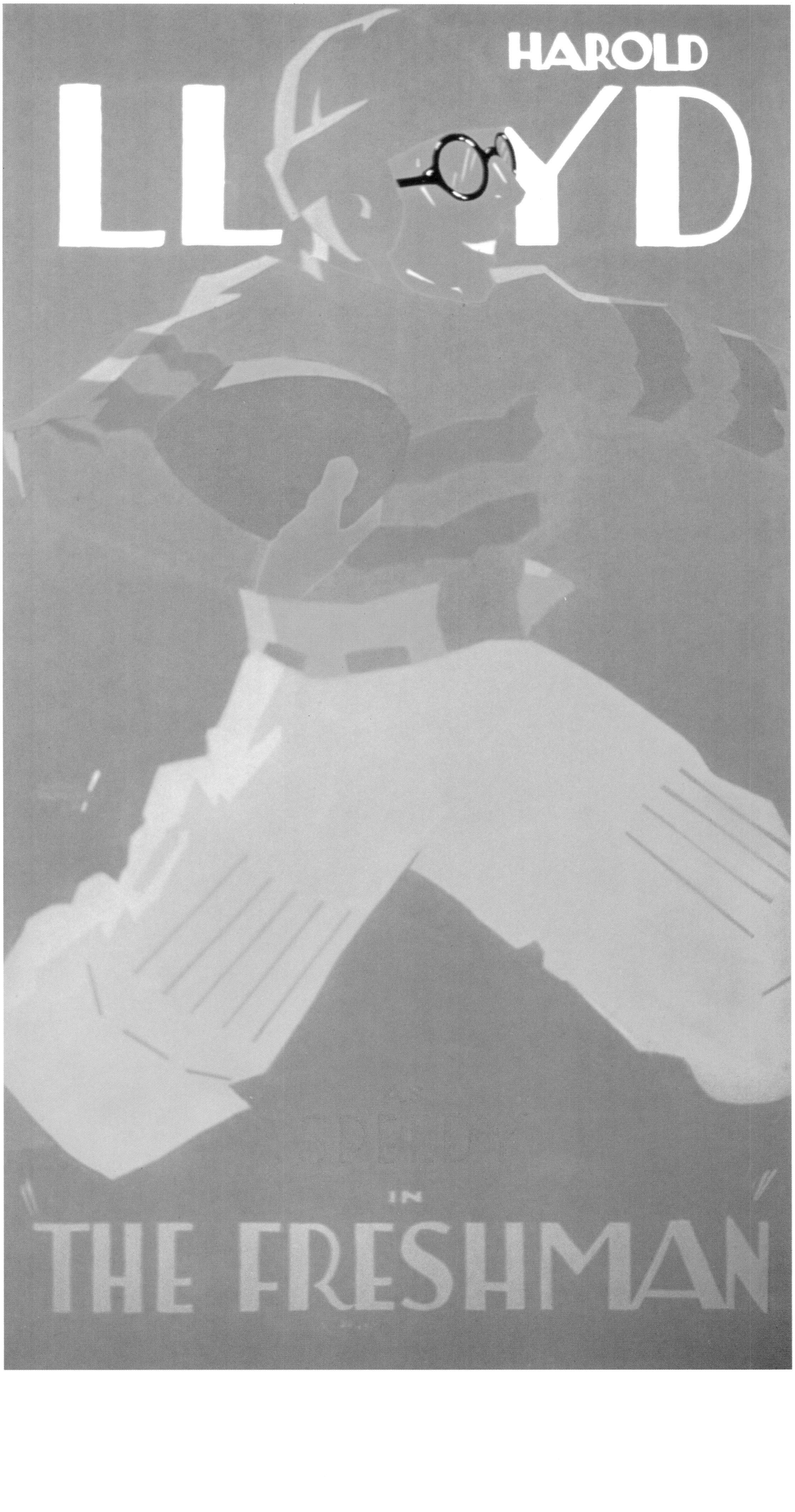
HAROLD
LLOYD
IN
THE FRESHMAN

Mysterious Lady

CAST

Greta Garbo, Conrad Nagel, Gustav von Seyffertitz

DIRECTOR

Fred Niblo

STUDIO

Metro-Goldwyn-Mayer Pictures

YEAR

1928

His Supreme Moment

CAST

Blanche Sweet, Ronald Colman, Kathlyn Myers

DIRECTOR

George Fitzmaurice

STUDIO

Samuel Goldwyn Productions/First National Pictures

YEAR

1925

Love

CAST
Greta Garbo, John Gilbert, George Fawcett, Emily Fitzroy

DIRECTOR
Edmund Goulding

STUDIO
Metro-Goldwyn-Mayer Pictures

YEAR
1927

John Gilbert

IN

LOVE
WITH
GRETA GARBO..

Monsieur Beaucaire

CAST
Rudolph Valentino, Bebe Daniels, Lois Wilson, Doris Kenyon

DIRECTOR
Sidney Olcott

STUDIO
Famous Players — Lasky/Paramount Pictures

YEAR
1924

RUDOLPH
VALENTINO
IN
BOOTH TARKINGTON'S ROMANCE
"Monsieur Beaucaire"

Quo Vadis?

CAST
Emil Jannings, Elena Sangro, Lillian Hall Davis

DIRECTOR
Gabriellino D'Annunzio, Georg Jacoby

STUDIO
Unione Cinématographica Italiana

YEAR
1925

Yolanda

CAST
Marion Davies, Lyn Harding, Holbrook Blinn, Leon Errol

DIRECTOR
Robert G. Vignola

STUDIO
Cosmopolitan Pictures/Metro-Goldwyn-Mayer Pictures

YEAR
1924

MARION DAVIES
IN

'YOLANDA'

Serenade

CAST
Adolphe Menjou, Kathryn Carver, Lawrence Grant

DIRECTOR
Harry D'Abbadie D'Arrast

STUDIO
Paramount Famous Lasky Corp.

YEAR
1927

ADOLPHE
MENJOU
IN
"SERENADE"

Lilac Time

CAST
Colleen Moore, Gary Cooper, Burr McIntosh, Kathryn McGuire

DIRECTOR
George Fitzmaurice

STUDIO
First National Pictures

YEAR
1928

COLLEEN
MOORE
IN
"LILAC TIME"
NOW PLAYING

Captain Blood

CAST

J. Warren Kerrigan, Jean Paige, Charlotte Merriam

DIRECTOR

David Smith

STUDIO

Vitagraph Co. of America

YEAR

1923

"CaptainBlood"

WITH

J. WARREN KERRIGAN AND JEAN PAIGE....

The Thundering Herd

CAST

Jack Holt, Lois Wilson, Noah Beery, Raymond Hatton

DIRECTOR

William Howard

STUDIO

Famous Players — Lasky/Paramount Pictures

YEAR

1925

BATISTE MADALENA
"THE THUNDERING HERD"
WITH
JACK HOLT, LOIS WILSON
NOAH BEERY
RAYMOND HATTON

The Night of Love

CAST
Ronald Colman, Vilma Banky, Montague Love, Sally Rand, Natalie Kingston

DIRECTOR
George Fitzmaurice

STUDIO
Samuel Goldwyn, Inc./United Artists

YEAR
1927

BATISTE
MADALENA
RONALD COLMAN
VILMA BANKY
IN
"The NIGHT
of LOVE"

Lovers

RAMON
NOVARRO
IN
"Lovers"

Service for Ladies

CAST
Adolphe Menjou, Kathryn Carver, Charles Lane, Lawrence Grant

DIRECTOR
Harry D'Abbadie D'Arrast

STUDIO
Paramount Famous Lasky Corp.

YEAR
1927

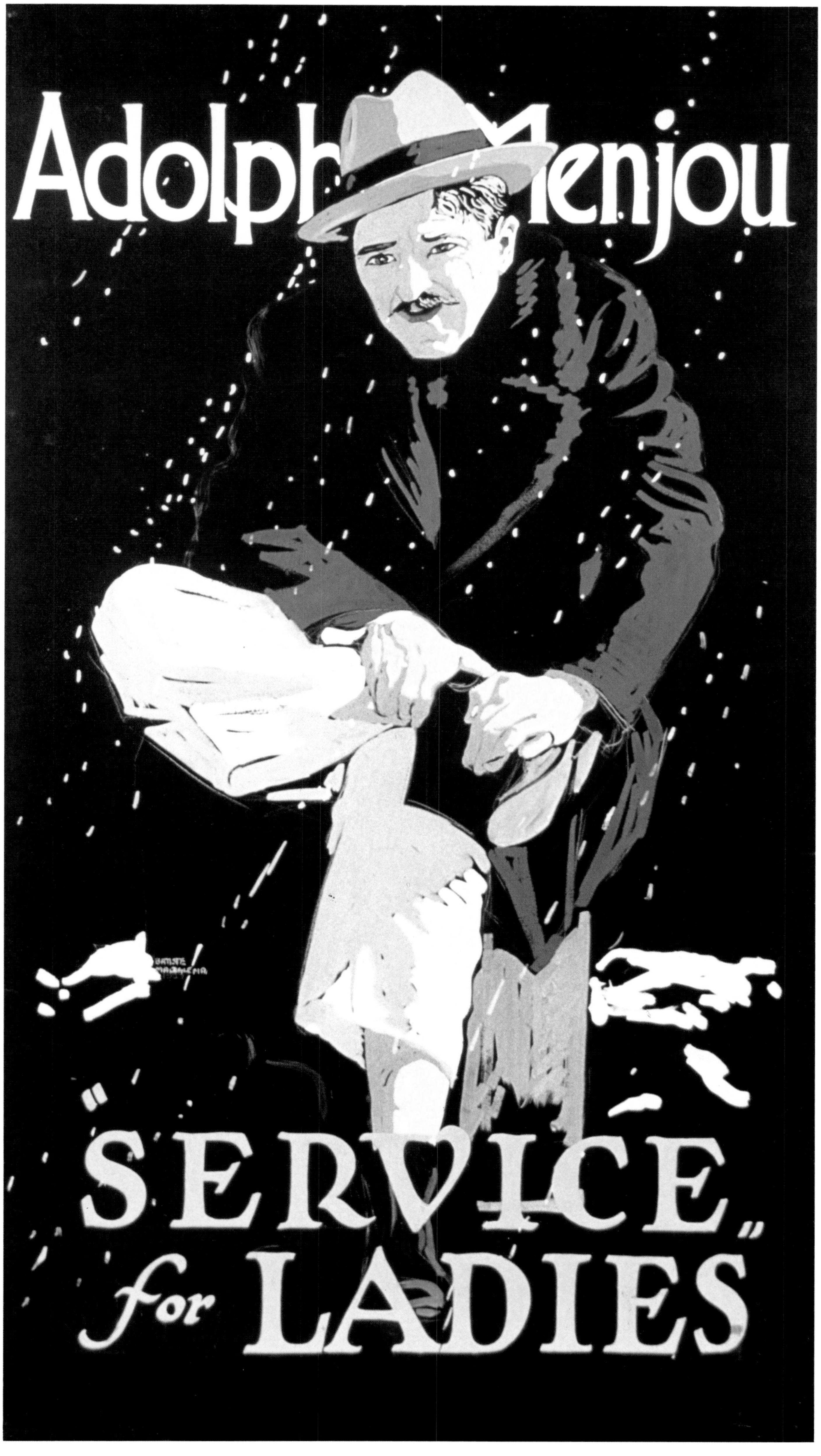
Adolph Menjou
"SERVICE for LADIES"

Wanderer of the Wasteland

CAST
Jack Holt, Kathlyn Williams, Billie Dove, Noah Beery

DIRECTOR
Irvin Willat

STUDIO
Famous Players — Lasky/Paramount Pictures

YEAR
1924

Rough House Rosie

CAST
Clara Bow, Reed Howes, Arthur Housman, Doris Hill

DIRECTOR
Frank Strayer

STUDIO
Paramount Famous Lasky Corp.

YEAR
1927

A COMEDY KNOCKOUT!

"ROUGH HOUSE ROSIE"

WITH

CLARA BOW

Sally of the Sawdust

CAST
W. C. Fields, Carol Dempster, Alfred Lunt

DIRECTOR
D.W. Griffith

STUDIO
D.W. Griffith, Inc./United Artists

YEAR
1925

The Lost World

CAST
Wallace Beery, Lewis Stone, Bessie Love, Lloyd Hughes

DIRECTOR
Harry O. Hoyt

STUDIO
First National Pictures

YEAR
1925

Little Annie Rooney

CAST
Mary Pickford, William Haines, Walter James

DIRECTOR
William Beaudine

STUDIO
Mary Pickford Co./United Artists

YEAR
1925

"OUR MARY"
AS PRINCESS
OF THE BOWERY
MARY
PICKFORD
IN
"LITTLE ANNIE ROONEY"

The Way of All Flesh

CAST
Emil Jannings, Belle Bennett, Phyllis Haver, Donald Keith

DIRECTOR
Victor Fleming

STUDIO
Paramount Famous Lasky Corp.

YEAR
1927

Clothes Make the Pirate

CAST
Leon Errol, Dorothy Gish, Nita Naldi, Tully Marshall

DIRECTOR
Maurice Tourneur

STUDIO
Sam E. Rork Productions/First National Pictures

YEAR
1925

The Ten Commandments

CAST
Theodore Roberts, Richard Dix, Leatrice Joy

DIRECTOR
Cecil B. DeMille

STUDIO
Famous Players — Lasky/Paramount Pictures

YEAR
1923

One of the most popular comedians of silent films inspired a poster in the artist's illustrative style

The Movie Posters

The famous deadpan comic is a woebegone soldier in Madalena's full-length portrait

BATISTE MADALENA
AN APPRECIATION

Anthony Slide

IN recent years our attitude toward the movie poster has shifted from one of attention to its informational value to appreciation of its artistic — and monetary — worth. This growing interest in the movie poster has spawned expensive art books, awards from at least one trade paper, and a multitude of eager dealers and collectors. What has yet to be established, however, is a body of scholarship concerning the posters' origins, their early creators, and the apparatus behind their design. Our view of the one-sheet as a mass-produced commodity has remained unchallenged. While occasionally a Thomas Hart Benton might have been hired to create a poster for *The Grapes of Wrath* or a Henry Clive to provide glamorous characterizations of major stars, generally the artist behind the poster has remained an anonymous employee of either the studio or the lithograph company — Water Color, Acme, J. H. Tooker, or H. C. Miner in New York, or Morgan and Otis in Cleveland.

Now all that has changed insofar as the poster art of one man is concerned. From the Eastman Theater in Rochester, New York, comes the work of Batiste Madalena, who between 1924 and 1928 created and hand-painted the posters — some 1,400 in all — advertising the films appearing at George Eastman's moving picture palace. In November 1919, *Photoplay* had described Eastman as "an extraordinary combination of great industrial builder and artist" — which perhaps explains his association with Madalena. No mass-produced artwork for the inventor of film stock, but rather individual and uniquely original pieces of art by a young local painter! How ironic that the only truly American art form, the motion picture, should — through the sponsorship of one of the industry's creators — have led to the birth of another American art form, the one-of-a-kind film poster.

There are so many styles employed in these posters that it is difficult to believe they are all the work of one artist. Of course, Art Deco, the popular style of the 1920s, is well represented, but so too are numerous others not as easily identifiable but no less distinctive. Madalena's versatility is readily apparent in the contrast between the simple, clean-cut, all-American illustrative style of the poster for *Spring Fever* and the subtly rendered phallic symbolism — something no censor-conscious studio artist would have dared — in the poster for Valentino's *Monsieur Beaucaire*. The artist's originality and inventiveness are apparent throughout the collection. For Harold Lloyd's *The Freshman*, Madalena exercised his imagination to arrive

Full-length figures and striking shadow play unify this eye-catching poster series

at a skillful collage to promote this story of a would-be football hero, achieving an effect impossible to equal in mass-duplicated studio art. Madalena is also a master of lettering; stylistically simple yet inventive, his lettering always serves the theme and design of the poster and the film, as in the *Beau Brummel* posters. Finally, Madalena's attention to detail — note the dappled shadows on the shadow sleeves of the character in *Captain Blood* — sets these hand-painted film posters above the transient medium of advertising art and places them in the aesthetic sphere of enduring values.

Madalena's paintings contravene movie poster convention not only in their style and design but also in their quixotic handling of stars and their billing. The British actor Ronald Colman, something of a matinee idol in his time, is given modest billing, and Marion Davies' image does not intrude upon an exquisitely delicate poster for *Yolanda*, while Ramon Novarro is given prominence beyond his fame. Valentino, naturally, "stars" in the posters for *The Son of the Sheik*, and Madalena always treats Lon Chaney with respect, relying upon the actor's features alone to identify him in several of the posters for *The Unknown*. But where no major stars are involved, as in *The Haunted House*, Madalena uses his poster to convey mood and theme simply but effectively; here he has emphasized the comedy–thriller aspect of the plot.

Perhaps best of all, Batiste Madalena's posters capture the glamour of an era in film history that is past and which no written word can adequately recapture. Most of the great films from the golden age of the silent film are represented here: the historical epics, such as *The Ten Commandments* and *The Wanderer*; the Westerns, such as *The Covered Wagon*; the romances, such as *Lilac Time*, *Love*, and *Monsieur Beaucaire*; and the comedies, such as *Rough House Rosie* and *The Freshman*. Also represented are the stars from an age when a star was a star, when audiences, through weekly visits to their local theaters, could spend an hour or two in close proximity to untouchable idols

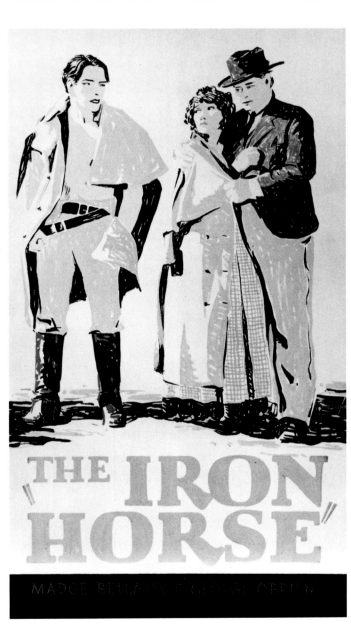

Dramatic scenes from The Iron Horse *lured moviegoers who hungered for adventure*

Richard Dix, a forgotten old favorite, was given star treatment in his glory days

such as Clara Bow, Valentino, Lon Chaney, and Garbo. Here are the remembered personalities — Keaton, Barrymore, and Lloyd — as well as the forgotten ones — J. Warren Kerrigan, Lya De Putti, and Richard Dix. Here, too, are those who disappeared with the coming of sound — Vilma Banky and Alma Rubens — and those who prospered — Adolphe Menjou, Joan Crawford, and Ronald Colman. The films were, for the most part, black-and-white, but it was a colorful age and somehow the vibrant hues and tones of these bright posters help to recreate it as much, if not more, than the films themselves. Tastes in films change, acting styles progress or evolve, but appreciation of art remains a constant.